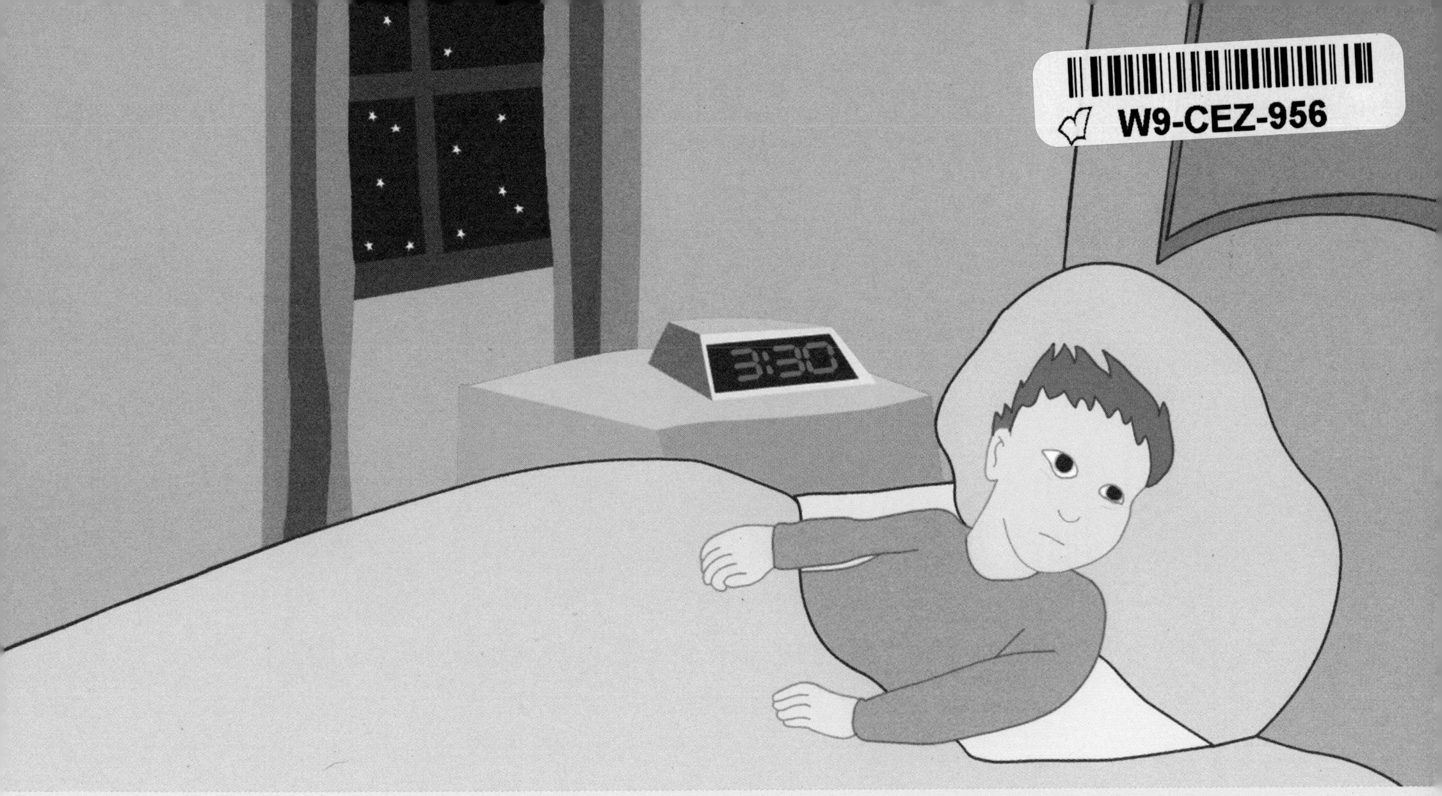

Pete can not sleep.

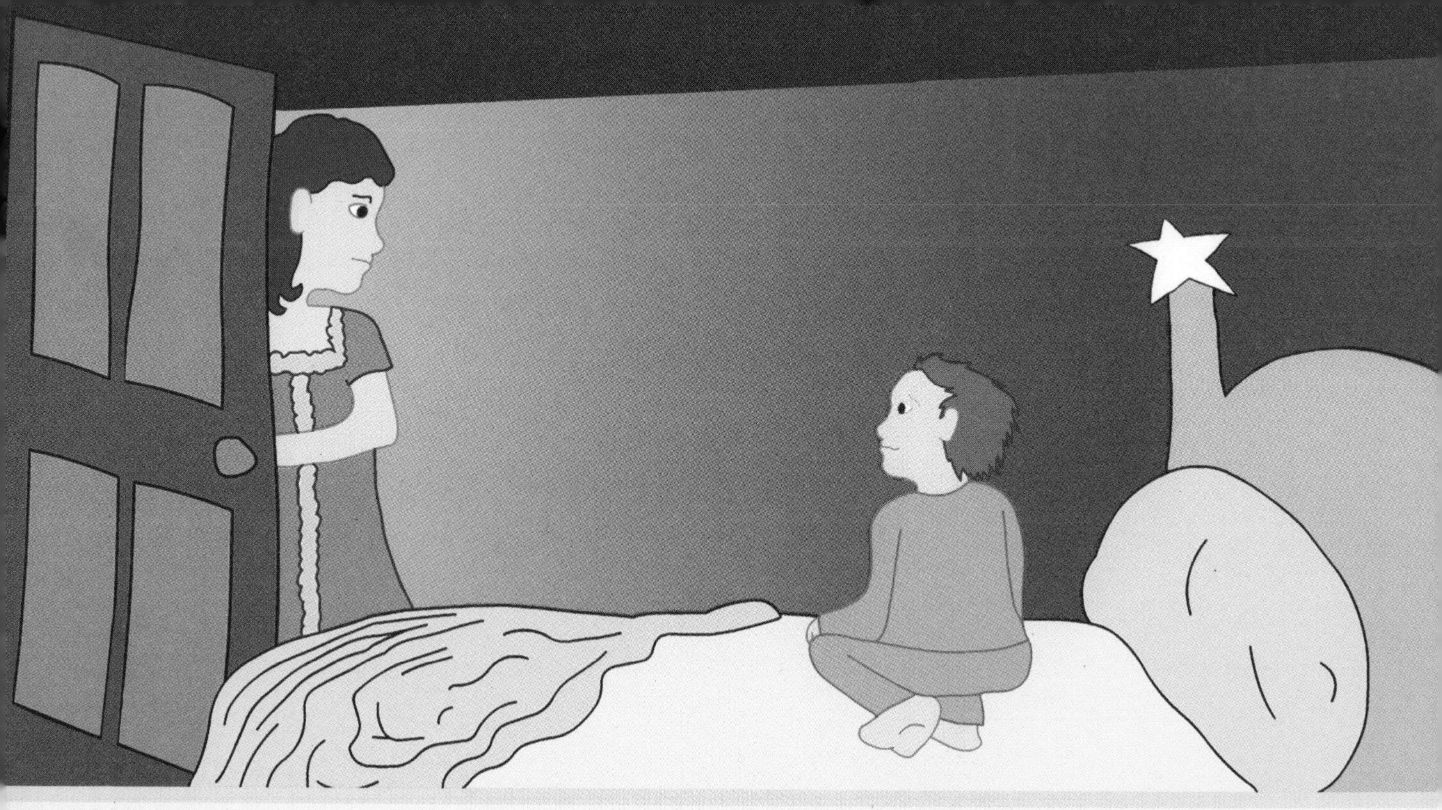

Pete needs help.

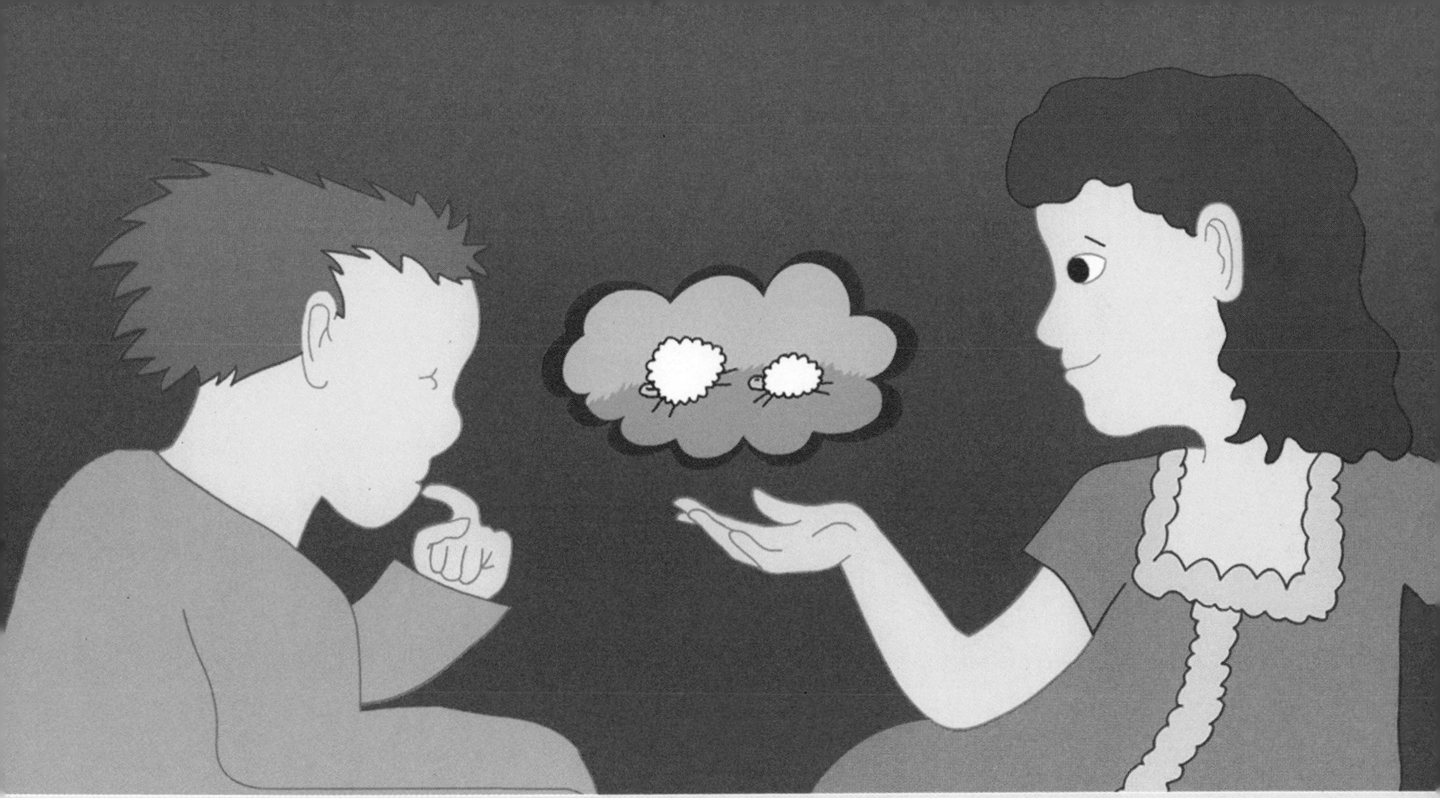

“Think of sheep,” says Mom.

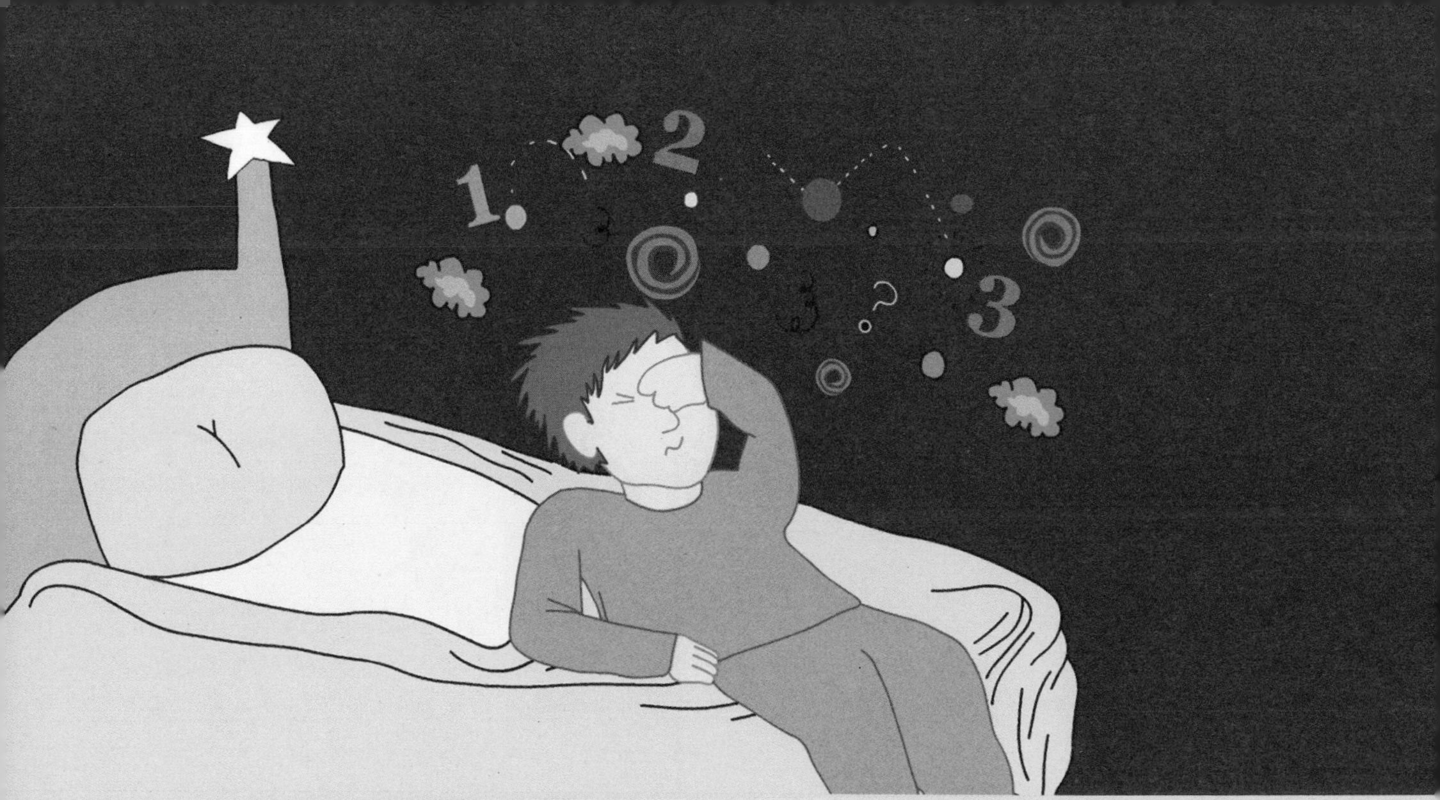

"One, two, three sheep,"
says Pete.

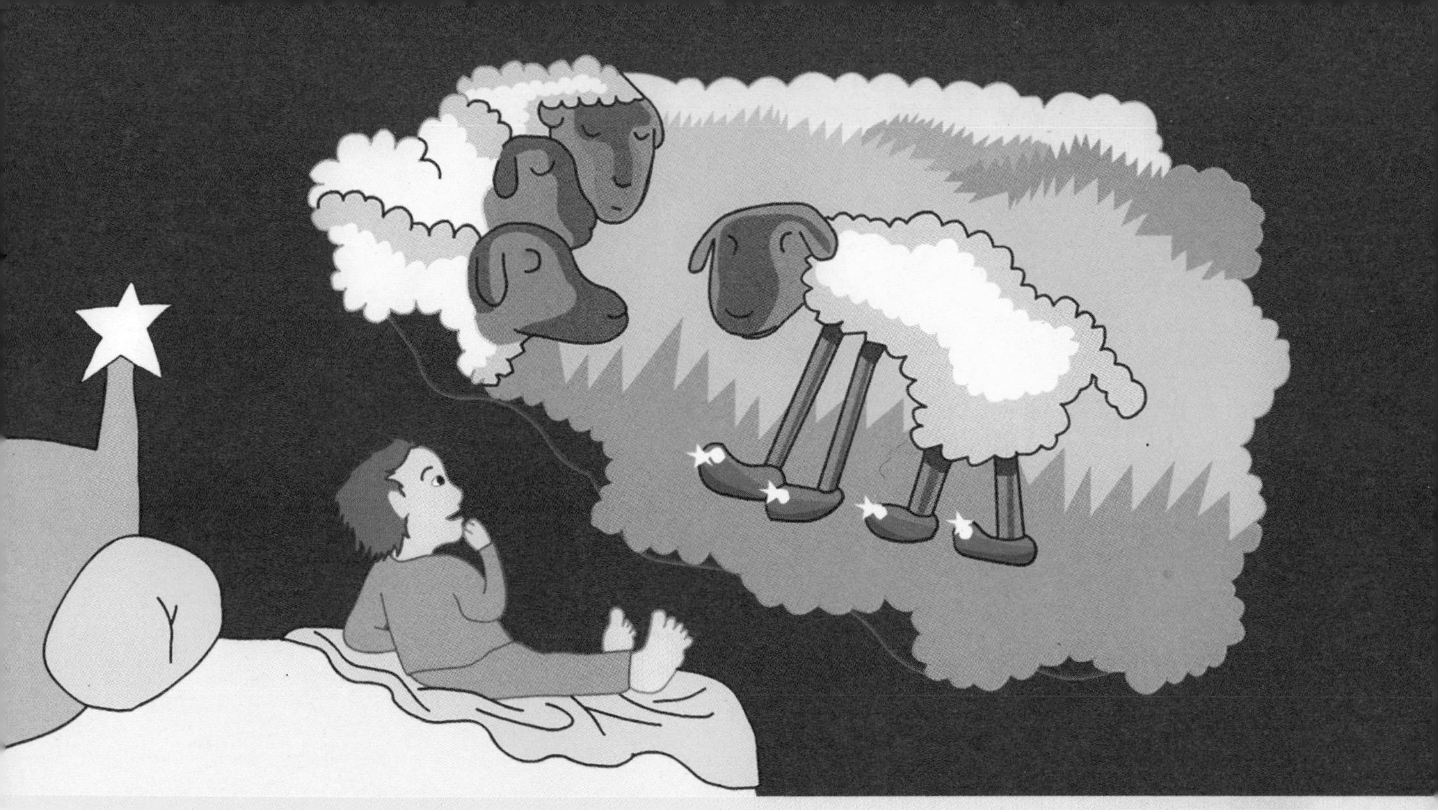

Then Pete sees sheep!

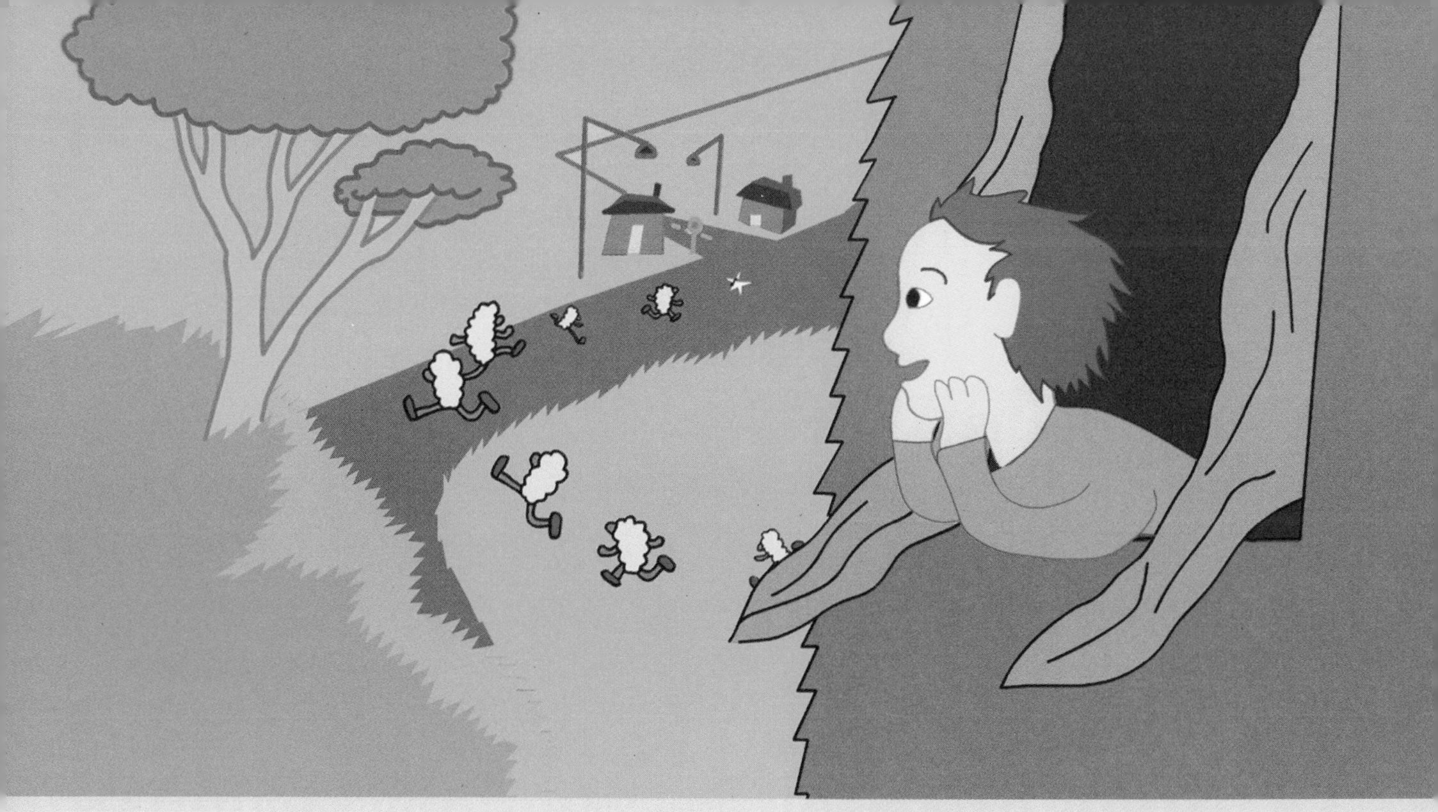

The sheep run past the tree!

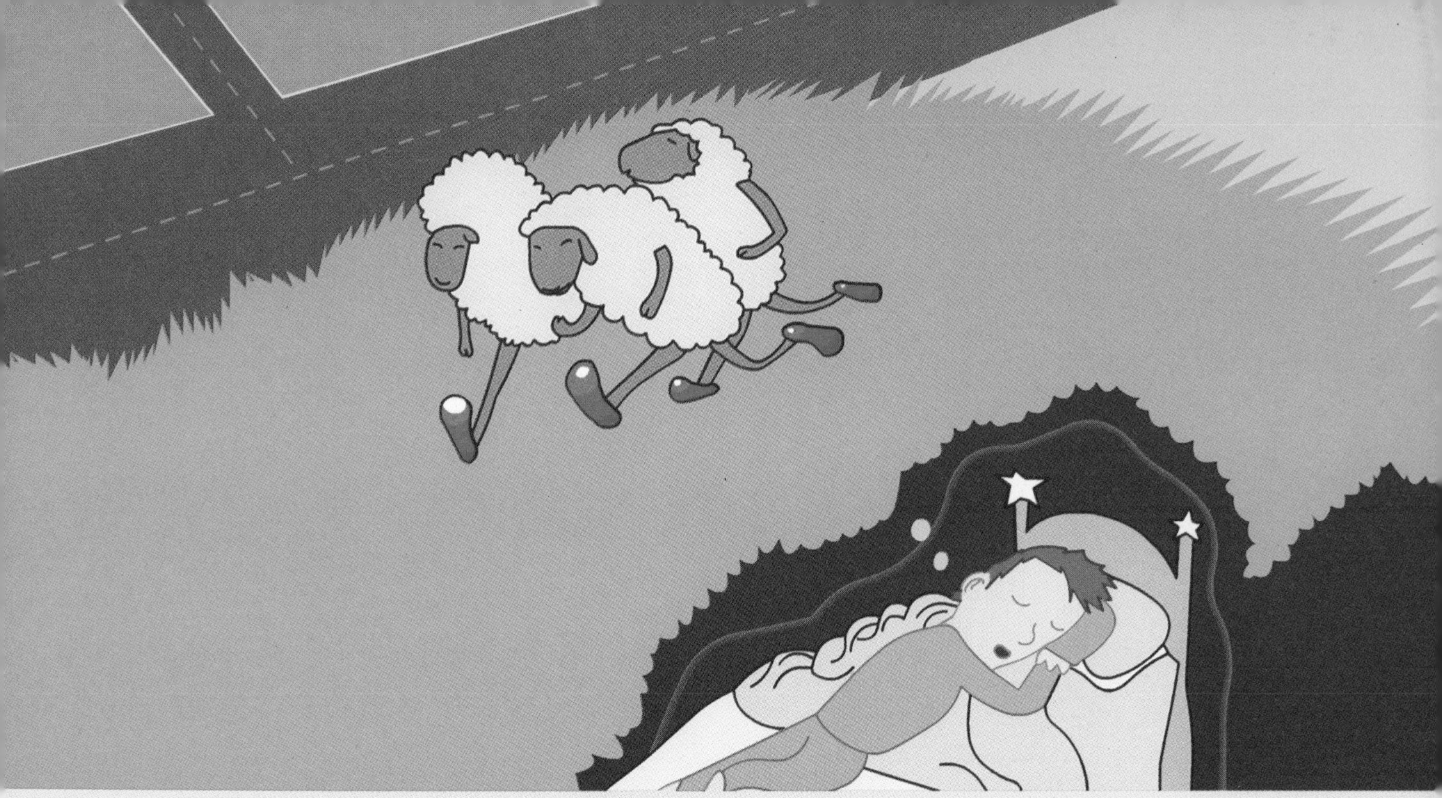

At last, Pete can sleep.

The end